MW00677152

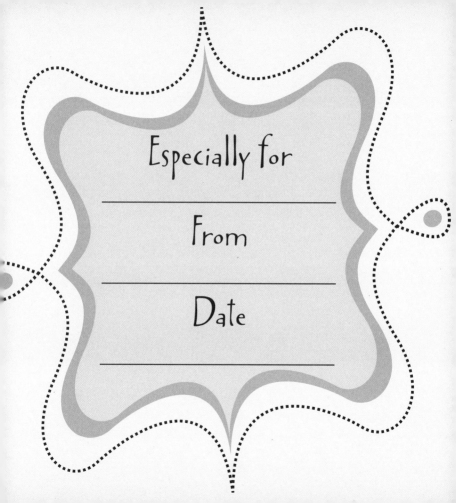

Especially for

_____

From

_____

Date

_____

© 2011 by Barbour Publishing, Inc.

Written and compiled by Ellyn Sanna.

ISBN 978-1-61626-318-8

All rights reserved. No part of this publication may be reproduced or transmitted for commercial purposes, except for brief quotations in printed reviews, without written permission of the publisher.

Scripture quotations marked CEV are from the Contemporary English Version Copyright © 1991, 1992, 1995 by American Bible Society, Used by permission.

Scripture quotations marked NIV are taken from the HOLY BIBLE, NEW INTERNATIONAL VERSION®. NIV®. Copyright 1973, 1978, 1984, 2010 by Biblica, Inc.™ Used by permission. All rights reserved worldwide.

Published by Barbour Publishing, Inc., P.O. Box 719, Uhrichsville, Ohio 44683, www.barbourbooks.com

Our mission is to publish and distribute inspirational products offering exceptional value and biblical encouragement to the masses.

Member of the
Evangelical Christian
Publishers Association

Printed in China.

power
of
positive parenting

BARBOUR
PUBLISHING

Introduction

Parenting. It's the most rewarding—and the hardest—job in the world! The good news is that no parent walks this road alone. Down through the centuries, from generation to generation, parents have experienced the same great joys alongside the same overwhelming challenges. They've left behind their thoughts, their wisdom, and their sense of humor, all as signposts for others to follow. And best of all, parents have a heavenly Parent who walks with them all the way, guiding and understanding. Where the love of human parents may fail, God's never will!

Making the decision to have a child—
it's momentous. It is to decide forever to have
your heart go walking outside your body.
ELIZABETH STONE

• • • • •

Before you were conceived, I wanted you.
Before you were born, I loved you.
Before you were here an hour, I would die
for you. This is the miracle of life.
MAUREEN HAWKINS

We worry about what a child will
become tomorrow; yet we forget
that he is someone today.
STACIA TAUSCHER

• • • • •

A child educated only at school
is an uneducated child.
GEORGE SANTAYANA

• • • • •

Home is the place where boys and girls first
learn how to limit their wishes, abide by rules,
and consider the rights and needs of others.
SIDONIE GRUENBERG

Even as the father lays down the law, he knows
that someday his children will break it. . . .
Terrible blunders will be made—disappointments
and failures, hurts and losses of every kind.
And they'll keep making them even after they've
found themselves too, of course, because
growing up is a process that goes on and on.
And every hard knock they ever get, knocks the
father even harder still, if that's possible, and
if and when they finally come through more or
less in one piece at the end, there's maybe no
rejoicing greater than his in all creation.

Frederick Buechner

A young child is, indeed, a true scientist,
just one big question mark. What? Why? How?
I never cease to marvel at the recurring miracle
of growth, to be fascinated by the mystery
and wonder of this brave enthusiasm.

Victoria Wagner

• • • • •

When I approach a child, he inspires in me
two sentiments; tenderness for what he is,
and respect for what he may become.

Louis Pasteur

Where did we ever get the crazy idea that in order to make children do better, first we have to make them feel worse? Think of the last time you felt humiliated or treated unfairly. Did you feel like cooperating or doing better?

JANE NELSON

• • • • •

Feelings of worth can flourish only in an atmosphere where individual differences are appreciated, mistakes are tolerated, communication is open, and rules are flexible— the kind of atmosphere that is found in a nurturing family.

VIRGINIA SATI

Children require guidance and
sympathy far more than instruction.
ANNIE SULLIVAN

If a child is to keep alive his inborn sense of wonder, he needs the companionship of at least one adult who can share it, rediscovering with him the joy, excitement, and mystery of the world we live in.

RACHEL CARSON

Nothing you do for children is ever wasted.
They seem not to notice us, hovering,
averting our eyes, and they seldom offer thanks,
but what we do for them is never wasted.
GARRISON KEILLOR

• • • • •

The old notion that children are the private
property of parents dies very slowly.
In reality, no parent raises a child alone.
MARIAN WRIGHT EDELMAN

It is not a bad thing that children
should occasionally, and politely,
put parents in their place.
COLETTE

• • • • •

You can learn many things from children.
How much patience you have, for instance.
FRANKLIN P. JONES

Bitter are the tears of a child:
Sweeten them.
Deep are the thoughts of a child:
Quiet them.
Sharp is the grief of a child:
Take it from him.
Soft is the heart of a child:
Do not harden it.
PAMELA GLENCONNER

Too often we give our children answers to remember rather than problems to solve.
ROGER LEWIN

• • • • •

The family is one of nature's masterpieces.
GEORGE SANTAYANA

May your father and mother rejoice;
may she who gave you birth be joyful!
PROVERBS 23:25 NIV

• • • • •

Children's children are a crown to the aged,
and parents are the pride of their children.
PROVERBS 17:6 NIV

Children have never been very good
at listening to their elders, but they
have never failed to imitate them.
JAMES BALDWIN

Govern a family as you would
cook a small fish—very gently.
CHINESE PROVERB

• • • • •

To put the world right in order, we must first
put the nation in order; to put the nation in
order, we must first put the family in order;
to put the family in order, we must first
cultivate our personal life; and to cultivate
our personal life, we must first set
our hearts right.
CONFUCIUS

To bring up a child in the way he should go,
travel that way yourself once in a while.
JOSH BILLINGS

• • • • •

Don't worry that children never listen to you;
worry that they are always watching you.
ROBERT FULGHUM

A parent's love is whole no matter
how many times divided.
ROBERT BRAULT

• • • • •

Each day of our lives we make deposits
in the memory banks of our children.
CHARLES R. SWINDOLL

Parenting is based far more on what you are (personal being and identity), than what you do (procedurally). If your spiritual identity is that of a Christ-one, a Christian; and if you are available to allow the very Being of the life of Jesus Christ to be lived out through you (behaviorally); then just "listen under" God in obedience and enjoy your children! Let them "see" and "catch" what God has for them through you.

JAMES A. FOWLER

Good, honest, hardheaded character is a function of the home. If the proper seed is sown there and properly nourished for a few years, it will not be easy for that plant to be uprooted.

GEORGE A. DORSEY

• • • • •

In bringing up children, spend on them half as much money and twice as much time.

UNKNOWN

A person soon learns how little he knows
when a child begins to ask questions.
RICHARD L. EVANS

• • • • •

Affirming words from moms and dads are like
light switches. Speak a word of affirmation at
the right moment in a child's life and it's like
lighting up a whole roomful of possibilities.
GARY SMALLEY

My son, keep your father's
command and do not forsake
your mother's teaching.
Bind them always on your heart;
fasten them around your neck.
PROVERBS 6:20–21 NIV

God sends children to enlarge our hearts
and make us unselfish and full of kindly
sympathies and affections.
MARY HOWITT

• • • • • •

Life affords no greater responsibility, no greater
privilege, than the raising of the next generation.
C. EVERETT KOOP, M.D.

It's not only children who grow. Parents do, too.
As much as we watch to see what our children do
with their lives, they are watching us to see what
we do with ours. I can't tell my children to reach
for the sun. All I can do is reach for it myself.

JOYCE MAYNARD

• • • • •

Lucky parents who have fine
children usually have lucky
children who have fine parents.

JAMES A. BREWER

When a child is born, a father is born. A mother is born, too, of course, but at least for her it's a gradual process. Body and soul, she has nine months to get used to what's happening. She becomes what's happening. But for even the best-prepared father, it happens all at once.
On the other side of a plate-glass window, a nurse is holding up something roughly the size of a loaf of bread for him to see for the first time. Even if he should decide to abandon it forever ten minutes later, the memory will nag him to the grave. He has seen the creation of the world. It has his mark on it. He has its mark on him. Both marks are, for better or for worse, indelible.

FREDERICK BUECHNER

The world talks to the mind. Parents speak
more intimately—they talk to the heart.
HAIM GINOTT

• • • • •

When you have children yourself, you begin
to understand what you owe your parents.
JAPANESE PROVERB

Affection without sentiment, authority without cruelty, discipline without aggression, humor without ridicule, sacrifice without obligation, companionship without possessiveness.

WILLIAM E. BLATZ

• • • • •

Before I got married I had six theories about bringing up children; now I have six children, and no theories.

JOHN WILMOT

The character and history of each child
may be a new and poetic experience
to the parent, if he will let it.
MARGARET FULLER

• • • • •

While we try to teach our children all about life,
our children teach us what life is all about.
ANGELA SCHWINDT

The essence of Christian parenting is the life of Jesus Christ lived out before our children. That expression of Christ's life cannot be orchestrated by techniques and procedures or by how-to formulas, but only as Christian parents are faithfully receptive to the divine dynamic of His activity.

JAMES A. FOWLER

Children learn to smile
from their parents.
SHINICHI SUZUKI

• • • • •

Let parents bequeath to their children not riches,
but the spirit of reverence.
PLATO

• • • • •

The best academy: a mother's knee.
JAMES LOWELL

If you raise your children to feel that they
can accomplish any goal or task they decide
upon, you will have succeeded as a parent,
and you will have given your children
the greatest of all blessings.
BRIAN TRACY

• • • • •

Your children will become what you are;
so be what you want them to be.
DAVID BLY

Your family and your love must be cultivated like a garden. Time, effort, and imagination must be summoned constantly to keep any relationship flourishing and growing.

JIM ROHN

• • • • •

If a child lives with acceptance and friendship, he learns to find love in the world.

DOROTHY LAW NEITE

Children seldom misquote you. In fact,
they usually repeat word for word
what you shouldn't have said.

UNKNOWN

● ● ● ● ●

My father didn't tell me how to live; he lived,
and let me watch him do it.

CLARENCE BUDINGTON KELLAND

The most assiduous task of parenting
is to divine the difference between
boundaries and bondage.

BARBARA KINGSOLVER

• • • • •

Children thrive when parents set
before them increasingly difficult,
but always meetable, challenges.

UNKNOWN

Children, obey your parents in the Lord, for this is right. "Honor your father and mother"—which is the first commandment with a promise—"so that it may go well with you and that you may enjoy long life on the earth." Fathers, do not exasperate your children; instead, bring them up in the training and instruction of the Lord.

EPHESIANS 6:1–4 NIV

I looked on childrearing not only as
a work of love and duty but as a
profession that was fully interesting and
challenging as any honorable profession
in the world and one that demanded
the best that I could bring to it.
ROSE KENNEDY

When you have brought up kids, there are
memories you store directly in your tear ducts.
ROBERT BRAULT

• • • • •

Parenthood: That state of being better
chaperoned than you were before marriage.
MARCELENE COX

• • • • •

What the child says, he has heard at home.
NIGERIAN PROVERB

The most important thing that parents can teach
their children is how to get along without them.
FRANK A. CLARK

• • • • •

Haste and hurry can only bear children
with many regrets along the way.
SENEGALESE PROVERB

Children will not remember you for the
material things you provided, but for
the feeling that you cherished them.
RICHARD EVANS

• • • • •

Family faces are. . .mirrors.
Looking at people who belong to us,
we see the past, present, and future.
GAIL LUMET BUCKLEY

• • • • •

By crawling, a child learns to stand.
WEST AFRICAN PROVERB

Honor your father and your mother
that you may live long in the land
the Lord *your God is giving you.*
Exodus 20:12 NIV

• • • • •

Mothers of families, even if they had a thousand
sons and daughters, would still find room for
every single one in their hearts, because that is
how true love works. It even seems that the more
children a mother has, the greater is her love
and care for each one individually.

Angela Merici

It is difficult to give children a
sense of security unless you
have it yourself. If you have it,
they catch it from you.
WILLIAM C. MENNINGER

The school will teach children how to read, but the environment of the home must teach them what to read. The school can teach them how to think, but the home must teach them what to believe.

Charles A. Wells

It would seem that something which means poverty, disorder, and violence every single day should be avoided entirely, but the desire to beget children is a natural urge.

PHYLLIS DILLER

• • • • •

Parenthood is not an object of appetite or even desire. It is an object of will. There is no appetite for parenthood; there is only a purpose or intention of parenthood.

ROBIN G. COLLINGWOOD

Children begin by loving their parents;
as they grow older they judge them;
sometimes they forgive them.

Oscar Wilde

• • • • •

There is only one pretty child in the world,
and every mother has it.

Chinese Proverb

How many hopes and fears, how many
ardent wishes and anxious apprehensions
are twisted together in the threads that
connect the parent with the child!

SAMUEL G. GOODRICH

• • • • •

Parents can plant magic in a child's mind
through certain words spoken with some
thrilling quality of voice, some uplift of
the heart and spirit.

ROBERT MACNEIL

Parents learn a lot from their children
about coping with life.
MURIEL SPARK

• • • • •

Of all nature's gifts to the human race,
what is sweeter to a man than his children?
MARCUS TULLIUS CICERO

• • • • •

*A woman giving birth to a child has pain
because her time has come; but when her baby
is born she forgets the anguish because of her
joy that a child is born into the world.*
JOHN 16:21 NIV

Our children's sorrows are often annoying to us as parents. That is because we feel we should be able to make our children always contented—and if they are not happy, then we have somehow failed. This is a lie, told to us by our culture. Children should be allowed their sorrows, their crabby moods, their disappointments. All humans have these feelings. But they are almost always not our problems as parents. In most cases, the best we can do is offer our sympathy and leave our children to figure out for themselves how to handle life's challenges on their own.

ABBIE TYNDALE

If your child is dancing clumsily, tell him:
"You are dancing clumsily"; do not tell him:
"Darling, do as you please."
TWI PROVERB

• • • • •

Our children need our affirmation. But they
also need our honesty. Loving correction is
based on reality, even when it is painful.
DACK JASON TAYTHORPE

A child who is to be successful is not to be reared exclusively on a bed of down.

AKAN PROVERB

• • • • •

Do not shield your child from all hardship and pain. One day you will not be there to take away the pain, no matter how much you wish you could be. Better that your child on that day be able to cope with it by himself. Allow him to learn.

HANFORD LYNDALE

If you can give your son or daughter
only one gift, let it be enthusiasm.
BRUCE BARTON

• • • • •

It is good to realize that if love and peace
can prevail on earth, and if we can teach our
children to honor nature's gifts, the joys and
beauties of the outdoors will be here forever.
JIMMY CARTER

The greatest natural resource that any country can have is its children.
DANNY KAYE

Once a child is born, it is no longer in our power not to love it nor care about it.

EPICTETUS

• • • • •

Loving a child is a circular business. . .the more you give, the more you get; the more you get, the more you want to give.

PENELOPE LEACH

• • • • •

A child is the root of the heart.

CAROLINA MARÍA DE JESÚS

Hear, O Israel: The LORD our God, the LORD is one. You shall love the LORD your God with all your heart and with all your soul and with all your might. And these words that I command you today shall be on your heart. You shall teach them diligently to your children, and shall talk of them when you sit in your house, and when you walk by the way, and when you lie down, and when you rise.

DEUTERONOMY 6:4–7 CEV

The best things you can give children,
next to good habits, are good memories.
SYDNEY J. HARRIS

• • • • •

Loving a child doesn't mean giving in to all his
whims; to love him is to bring out the best in
him, to teach him to love what is difficult.
NADIA BOULANGER

A child who is carried on the back
will not know how far the journey is.
NIGERIAN PROVERB

• • • • •

When I was a child, my father insisted that we
children walk through the deep snow when
we went into town with him. When my mother
wanted him to carry us or pull us on the sled,
he said no, the walk would make us strong.
But he always let us walk in his footsteps.
GREGORY MAKEPEACE

What you help a child to love can be more important than what you help him to learn.

AFRICAN PROVERB

● ● ● ● ●

My mother took me into the fields and woods from the time I was a tiny thing. From her I learned the names of flowers and trees and birds—but more important, I learned to love Nature, to hear God's voice in the songs of birds and the sigh of the wind in the leaves.

MORTON PHILLIPS

I learned to sing before I could talk. This was the gift my mother gave me. My mother could not speak her feelings in words—but she could sing. From her, I learned that music was another language, a language that God understood.
CYNTHIA TERWILLIGER

• • • • •

A child brought up where there is always dancing cannot fail to dance.
NYANJA PROVERB

Having a child fall asleep in your arms is
one of the most peaceful feelings in the world.
ANDY ROONEY

• • • • • •

We find delight in the beauty and
happiness of children that makes
the heart too big for the body.
RALPH WALDO EMERSON

We cannot fashion our children after our desires;
we must have them and love them as
God has given them to us.
JOHANN WOLFGANG VON GOETHE

• • • • •

Children need models rather than critics.
JOSEPH JOUBERT

Many things can wait; the child cannot.
Now is the time his bones are being formed,
his mind is being developed. To him we cannot
say tomorrow; his name is today.

GABRIELA MISTRAL

· · · · · ·

Listen, my son, to your father's instruction
and do not forsake your mother's teaching.
They are a garland to grace your head
and a chain to adorn your neck.

PROVERBS 1:8–9 NIV

The family is both the fundamental unit of society as well as the root of culture. It. . .is a perpetual source of encouragement, advocacy, assurance, and emotional refueling that empowers a child to venture with confidence into the greater world and to become all that he can be.

MARIANNE E. NEIFERT

• • • • •

Raising kids is part joy
and part guerilla warfare.

ED ASNER

Children are natural mimics:
they act like their parents in spite of every
attempt to teach them good manners.
UNKNOWN

There is always a moment in
childhood when the door opens
and lets the future in.
GRAHAM GREEN

The deeds of the children are a testament to the upbringing they received from their parents.
CHRISTOPHER PAOLINI

• • • • •

When you bear a grudge,
your child will also bear a grudge.
RWANDESE PROVERB

• • • • •

If a mother steals with a child strapped in the back, what do you expect of the child?
AFRICAN PROVERB

I know how sobering and exhausting parenthood is. But the reality is that our children's future depends on us as parents. Because we know that the first years truly last forever.

ROB REINER

• • • • • •

Start children off on the way they should go, and even when they are old they will not turn from it.
PROVERBS 22:6 NIV

• • • • • •

Every word and deed of a parent is a fiber woven into the character of a child, which ultimately determines how that child fits into the fabric of society.
DAVID WILKERSON

Train your child in the way you know
you should have gone yourself.
CHARLES HADDON SPURGEON

• • • • •

Parenthood remains the greatest
single preserve of the amateur.
ALVIN TOFFLER

• • • • •

The best brought-up children are those
who have seen their parents as they are.
Hypocrisy is not the parents' first duty.
GEORGE BERNARD SHAW

Motherhood is like planting sequoia trees.
You have to wait a long time to
find out how you've done.
H. JACKSON BROWN JR.

• • • • •

Stories first heard at a mother's knee are never
wholly forgotten—a little spring that never quite
dries up in our journey through scorching years.
GIOVANNI RUFFINI

There is religion in all deep love, but the love of
a mother is the veil of a softer light, between the
heart and the heavenly Father.

SAMUEL TAYLOR COLERIDGE

• • • • •

The soul is healed by being with children.

FYODOR DOSTOEVSKY

Parenting is one of the most challenging, demanding, and stressful jobs on the planet. It is also one of the most important, for how it is done influences in great measure the heart and soul and consciousness of the next generation.

MYLA AND JON KABAT-ZINN

• • • • •

Tell it to your children, and let your children tell it to their children, and their children to the next generation.

JOEL 1:3 NIV

When Jesus Christ is allowed to function in the family, and His life is lived out through the parent, then we will see the family function as God designed it to function; not by formula, but by faith which is the receptivity of His activity.

JAMES A. FOWLER

Choosing to have a baby is not simply within our power. We can open up that possibility, we can go a long way towards enabling it to happen, but we cannot dictate it. In the end, it is God who gives life.

MARGARET HEBBLETHWAITE

My son, keep my words and store up my commands within you. Keep my commands and you will live; guard my teachings as the apple of your eye. Bind them on your fingers; write them on the table of your heart.

PROVERBS 7:1–3 NIV

The trouble with the family is that children
grow out of childhood, but parents
never grow out of parenthood.
EVAN ESAR

• • • • •

If you would have your son to walk honorably
through the world, you must not attempt to clear
the stones from his path, but teach him to walk
firmly over them—not insist upon leading him by
the hand, but let him learn to go alone.
ANNE BRONTË

Bless your children with the gift of yourself.
You do this by living in harmony with the best and
truest version of yourself, the person God calls
you to be. This is a challenge, but it is the best
way to bless your children—and it is a blessing
that will lift your own heart closer to God.

Adam Brown Hunter

• • • • • •

Outstanding parents not only acknowledge
their children's dreams, but also
seek a path to their reality.

Wes Fessler

There is no greater leadership
challenge than parenting.
JIM ROHN

• • • • •

The more people have studied different methods
of bringing up children, the more they have
come to the conclusion that what good mothers
and fathers instinctively feel like doing for their
babies is the best after all.
BENJAMIN SPOCK

I talk and talk and talk, and I haven't taught people in fifty years what my father taught by example in one week.
MARIO CUOMO

• • • • •

Patience is the mother of a beautiful child.
BANTU PROVERB

The most important thing a father
can do for his children is to love their
mother; and the most important thing
a mother can do for her children
is to love their father.
UNKNOWN

Becoming a father. . .sets in motion the forces that in time will alter consciousness, self-perception, and even attitude toward the outside world.

LIBBY COLMAN

• • • • •

The everyday miracle of birth changed my orientation in life. . . . I felt at once whole and broken, fulfilled and empty, vibrant with life and sorely wounded.

NAOMI RUTH LOWINSKI

The truth is we are bound to fail our children by our own human limitations. We need to be people as well as mothers; we will always be balancing our own needs against those of others. We are certain to err on the side of too much or too little control, discipline, love, support, attention, money. We are doomed to fail the ones we love the most.

NAOMI RUTH LOWINSKI

● ● ● ● ●

Our parents always fail us. . . . Why is this so? Because they are limited human beings; and for the same reason we, too, will fail our children.

LARRY JAFFEE

Many a parent has come to that exasperating point where they cry out, "God, unless You do something in this family, it is going to be a total fiasco and failure!" God loves to hear that cry, for then He can begin to function as He desires.

JAMES A. FOWLER

We as parents are here to encourage our
children to explore the world, learn and see new
things. We give them courage and confidence,
but ultimately it is up to them to take off without
us, doing their best, finishing well, knowing that
if they need us, we are never far behind.

UNKNOWN

• • • • •

If you talk to your children, you can help them
to keep their lives together. If you talk to them
skillfully, you can help them to build future dreams.

JIM ROHN

I will open my mouth with a parable;
I will utter hidden things, things from of old—
things we have heard and known,
things our ancestors have told us.
We will not hide them from their descendants;
we will tell the next generation
the praiseworthy deeds of the LORD,
his power, and the wonders he has done. . .
which he commanded our ancestors
to teach their children,
so the next generation would know them,
even the children yet to be born,
and they in turn would tell their children.
Then they would put their trust in God
and would not forget his deeds
but would keep his commands.
PSALM 78:2–7 NIV

Leadership is the great challenge of the twenty-first century in science, politics, education, and industry. But the greatest challenge in leadership is parenting. We need to do more than just get our enterprises ready for the challenges of the twenty-first century. We also need to get our children ready for the challenges of the twenty-first century.

JIM ROHN

Parents are to engage in guiding the child through the preliminaries of the course of life, admitting throughout that they are just trying to learn where the course goes, at the same time as the child is. We are not God! And we do not have it all figured out! We are there to assist them in getting a good start.

JAMES A. FOWLER

For only as we ourselves, as adults, actually move and have our being in the state of love, can we be appropriate models and guides for our children. What we are teaches the child far more than what we say, so we must be what we want our children to become.

JOSEPH CHILTON PEARCE

As adults, we must ask more of our children than they know how to ask of themselves. What can we do to foster their open-hearted hopefulness, engage their need to collaborate, be an incentive to utilize their natural competency and compassion. . .show them ways they can connect, reach out, weave themselves into the web of relationships that is called community.

DAWNA MARKOVA

To understand your parents' love,
you must raise children yourself.
CHINESE PROVERB

•   •   •   •   •

To be in your children's memories tomorrow,
you have to be in their lives today.
UNKNOWN

•   •   •   •   •

A mother understands what a child does not say.
JEWISH PROVERB

A baby will make love stronger, days shorter, nights longer, bankroll smaller, home happier, clothes shabbier, the past forgotten, and the future worth living for.

UNKNOWN

• • • • •

A man never stands as tall as when he kneels to help a child.

PYTHAGORAS

Stop trying to perfect your child, but keep trying to perfect your relationship with him.

Dr. Henker

• • • • •

As your kids grow, they may forget what you said but won't forget how you made them feel.

Kevin Heath

*Praise the L*ORD*! Blessed are those who fear the*
*L*ORD*, who find great delight in his commands.*
Their children will be mighty in the land;
the generation of the upright will be blessed.
PSALM 112:1–2 NIV

• • • • •

Kids learn integrity from us: Integrity is what we
say, what we do, and what we say we do.
DON GALER

Children are apt to live up to
what you believe of them.
LADY BIRD JOHNSON

• • • • •

If your child has a weakness,
teach them how to turn it into a strength!
The only failure is not trying.
KEVIN HEATH

If you want your children to improve,
let them overhear the nice things
you say about them to others.
HAIM GINOTT

• • • • •

Children desperately need to know—and to hear
in ways they understand and remember—
that they're loved and valued by Mom and Dad.
PAUL SMALLY

• • • • •

The art of mothering is to teach
the art of living to children.
ELAINE HEFFNER

All parents should know that he
who knows patience knows peace.
CHINESE PROVERB

• • • • •

Communicating with kids, it's a two-way street.
Sometimes they just need us to be there
for them and listen.
KEVIN HEATH

Love and respect are the most important aspects
of parenting, and of all relationships.
JODIE FOSTER

• • • • •

Teach your children: You have many choices.
You can choose forgiveness over revenge,
joy over despair. You can choose
action over apathy.
STEPHANIE MARSTON

When you give a little of yourself to a child,
you give a little of yourself to their future!
KEVIN HEATH

• • • • •

By profession I am a soldier and take pride in
that fact, but I am prouder to be a father.
GENERAL DOUGLAS MACARTHUR

Encourage your kids to dream. Imagination
will often carry us to worlds that never were.
But without it we go nowhere.
Carl Sagan

•   •   •   •   •

It is time for parents to teach young people that
in diversity there is beauty and there is strength.
Maya Angelou

Parents need to listen as much
as their kids do to them:
The first duty of love is to listen.
PAUL TILLICH

Praise your children openly,
reprehend them secretly.
W. CECIL

• • • • •

Live so that when your children think of fairness
and integrity, they think of you.
H. JACKSON BROWN JR.

If I had my child to raise over again:
I'd build self-esteem first and the house later.
I'd finger paint more and point the finger less.
I would do less correcting and more connecting.
I'd take my eyes off my watch
and watch with my eyes.
I would care to know less and
know to care more. . . .
I'd model less about the love of power
and more about the power of love.

DIANE LOOMANS

Family life is too intimate to be preserved by the spirit of justice. It can be sustained by a spirit of love which goes beyond justice.

REINHOLD NIEBUHR

• • • • •

He that raises a large family does, indeed, while he lives to observe them, stand a broader mark for sorrow; but then he stands a broader mark for pleasure, too.

BENJAMIN FRANKLIN

By the grace God has given me, I laid a foundation as a wise builder, and someone else is building on it. But each one should build with care. For no one can lay any foundation other than the one already laid, which is Jesus Christ. If anyone builds on this foundation using gold, silver, costly stones, wood, hay or straw, their work will be shown for what it is, because the Day will bring it to light. It will be revealed with fire, and the fire will test the quality of each person's work.

1 CORINTHIANS 3:10–14 NIV

The family is the cornerstone of our society. More than any other force it shapes the attitude, the hopes, the ambitions, and the values of the child. And when the family collapses, it is the children that are usually damaged. When it happens on a massive scale, the community itself is crippled. So, unless we work to strengthen the family, to create conditions under which most parents will stay together, all the rest—schools, playgrounds, and public assistance, and private concern—will never be enough.

LYNDON BAINES JOHNSON

Family quarrels have a total bitterness
unmatched by others. Yet it sometimes
happens that they also have a kind of tang,
a pleasantness beneath the unpleasantness,
based on the tacit understanding that this is not
for keeps; that any limb you climb out on will still
be there later for you to climb back.
MIGNON MCLAUGHLIN

Family life is full of major and minor crises—
the ups and downs of health, success and failure
in career, marriage, and divorce—and all kinds
of characters. It is tied to places and events and
histories. With all of these felt details, life etches
itself into memory and personality. It's difficult to
imagine anything more nourishing to the soul.

THOMAS MOORE

A family is a unit composed not only of children
but of men, women, an occasional animal,
and the common cold.

OGDEN NASH

• • • • •

In thinking, keep to the simple. In conflict, be fair
and generous. In governing, don't try to control.
In work, do what you enjoy. In family life,
be completely present.

LAO TZU

A family is a place where principles
are hammered and honed on
the anvil of everyday living.
CHARLES SWINDOLL

• • • • •

Family life! The United Nations is child's play
compared to the tugs and splits and need to
understand and forgive in any family.
MARY SARTON

Our children will grow up and leave us parents—but we will still share a common language, one we created together on family vacations and Christmas mornings, during that long horrible winter when we all had the flu, and at the dinner table down through the years. We will not lose that link.

LAVENDER JAMES

In family life, love is the oil that eases friction,
the cement that binds closer together,
and the music that brings harmony.
EVA BURROWS

• • • • •

In every dispute between parent and child,
both cannot be right, but they may be, and
usually are, both wrong. It is this situation which
gives family life its peculiar hysterical charm.
ISAAC ROSENFELD

In every conceivable manner, the family
is link to our past, bridge to our future.
ALEX HALEY

• • • • •

I know why families were created with all
their imperfections. They humanize you.
They are made to make you forget yourself
occasionally, so that the beautiful balance
of life is not destroyed.
ANAIS NIN

Families are the compass that guides us.
They are the inspiration to reach great heights
and our comfort when we occasionally falter.
BRAD HENRY

• • • • •

Bringing up a family should be an adventure,
not an anxious discipline in which everybody
is constantly graded for performance.
MILTON R. SAPERSTEIN

Then our sons in their youth will be like well-nurtured plants, and our daughters will be like pillars carved to adorn a palace.
PSALM 144:12 NIV

• • • • •

Whoever fears the LORD has a secure fortress, and for their children it will be a refuge.
PROVERBS 14:26 NIV

• • • • •

Your Father in heaven is not willing that any of these little ones should perish.
MATTHEW 18:14 NIV

At the end of the day, a loving family should find everything forgivable.
MARK V. OLSEN AND WILL SHEFFER

• • • • •

A man travels the world over in search of what he needs, and returns home to find it.
GEORGE MOORE

Other things may change us,
but we start and end with the family.
ANTHONY BRANDT

• • • • •

The only rock I know that stays steady, the only
institution I know that works is the family.
LEE IACOCCA

• • • • •

In time of test, family is best.
BURMESE PROVERB

The great gift of family life is to be intimately
acquainted with people you might never even
introduce yourself to, had life not done it for you.
KENDALL HAILEY

• • • • • •

The family—that dear octopus from whose
tentacles we never quite escape, nor,
in our inmost hearts, ever quite wish to.
DODIE SMITH

• • • • •

The happiest moments of my life have
been the few which I have passed at
home in the bosom of my family.
THOMAS JEFFERSON

The great advantage of living in a large family is that early lesson of life's essential unfairness.
NANCY MITFORD

• • • • •

Call it a clan, call it a network, call it a tribe, call it a family. Whatever you call it, whoever you are, you need one.
JANE HOWARD

• • • • •

To us, family means putting your arms around each other and being there.
BARBARA BUSH

The happiness of the domestic fireside is the first boon of Heaven; and it is well it is so, since it is that which is the lot of the mass of mankind.

THOMAS JEFFERSON

• • • • •

You don't choose your family. They are God's gift to you, as you are to them.

DESMOND TUTU

Families are like fudge—
mostly sweet, with a few nuts.
UNKNOWN

• • • • •

It is not flesh and blood but the heart
which makes us fathers and sons.
JOHANN SCHILLER

• • • • •

At the critical juncture in all human
relationships, there is only one question,
"What would love do now?"
NEALE DONALD WALSCH

If you only have one smile in you,
give it to the people you love.
MAYA ANGELOU

• • • • •

The informality of family life is a blessed
condition that allows us to become our
best while looking our worst.
MARGE KENNEDY

• • • • •

If it is desirable that our children be kind,
responsible, pleasant, and honest, then those
qualities must be taught—not hoped for.
JAMES DOBSON

Our greatest obligation to our children is
to prepare them to understand and to deal
effectively with the world in which they will live
and not with the world we have known or the
world we would prefer to have.

GRAYSON KIRK

I have no greater joy than
to hear that my children
are walking in the truth.
3 JOHN 1:4 NIV

Foster independence among your children.
Encourage them to cook, clean, and contribute.
BRIAN TRACY

• • • • •

It's the little things you do day in and day out that
count. That's the way you teach your children.
AMANDA PAYS

Children are like wet cement.
Whatever falls on them makes an impression.
HAIM GINOTT

• • • • •

Parents who are afraid to put their foot down
usually have children who step on their toes.
ASIAN PROVERB

Raising children is a creative endeavor,
an art, rather than a science.
BRUNO BETTELHEIM

• • • • •

Parents are the first teachers of the children.
BURMESE PROVERB

Perhaps parents would enjoy their children
more if they stopped to realize that the film of
childhood can never be run through
for a second showing.
EVELYN NOWN

● ● ● ● ●

Do not confine your children to your own
learning, for they were born in another time.
HEBREW PROVERB

You have a lifetime to work,
but children are only young once.
POLISH PROVERB

• • • • •

If you bungle raising your children, I don't think
whatever else you do well matters very much.
JACQUELINE KENNEDY ONASSIS

There is a wonderful word—
Why?—that children, all children
use. When they stop using it, the
reason too often is that no one bothered
to answer them. No one focused and
cultivated the child's innate sense
of the adventure of life.
ELEANOR ROOSEVELT

Remember that your children are not your own,
but are lent to you by the Creator.
NATIVE AMERICAN PROVERB

• • • • •

You don't know how much you don't know
until your children grow up and tell you
how much you don't know.
S. J. PERELMAN

Life, love, and laughter—what priceless
gifts to give our children.
PHYLLIS CAMPBELL DRYDEN

• • • • •

What you leave in your children is more
important than what you leave to them.
DENIS WAITLEY

• • • • •

No commitment in the whole world demands
quite as much as bringing up children.
JANENE WOLSEY BAADSGAARD

We want our children to grow up to be such persons that ill-fortune, if they meet with it, will bring out strength in them, and that good fortune will not trip them up, but make them winners.

EDWARD SANDFORD MARTIN

• • • • • •

You can never protect children from the vicissitudes of life. Children will learn from the bad experiences as well as the good. The point is these experiences should not be engineered by us out of some false sense that we're creating them for the child's benefit. Life itself has enough goods and bads without our having to manufacture them.

DAVID ELKIND

Don't be discouraged if your children reject your advice. Years later they will offer it to their own offspring.

UNKNOWN

• • • • •

Don't set your wit against a child.

JONATHAN SWIFT

• • • • •

Every generation revolts against its fathers and makes friends with its grandfathers.

LEWIS MUMFORD

Fathers and mothers have lost the idea
that the highest aspiration they might
have for their children is for them to
be wise. . .specialized competence and
success are all that they can imagine.
ALLAN BLOOM

*Unless the LORD builds the house,
its builders labor in vain.*
PSALM 127:1 NIV

• • • • • •

*She watches over the affairs of her household
and does not eat the bread of idleness.*
PROVERBS 31:27 NIV

• • • • • •

*For God is not a God of
disorder but of peace.*
1 CORINTHIANS 14:33 NIV

There is no friendship, no love,
like that of the parent for the child.
HENRY WARD BEECHER

· · · · ·

Romance fails us and so do friendships,
but the relationship of parent and child, less
noisy than all the others, remains indelible and
indestructible, the strongest relationship on earth.
THEODORE REIK

· · · · ·

Always kiss your children goodnight—
even if they're already asleep.
H. JACKSON BROWN JR.

A baby is God's opinion that
the world should go on.
CARL SANDBURG

• • • • •

A father is someone who carries pictures
where his money used to be.
UNKNOWN

Whatever they grow up to be, they are still our children, and the one most important of all the things we can give to them is unconditional love. Not a love that depends on anything at all except that they are our children.

ROSALEEN DICKSON

• • • • •

No matter what you've done for yourself or for humanity, if you can't look back on having given love and attention to your own family, what have you really accomplished?

ELBERT HUBBARD

Children in a family are like flowers in a bouquet: there's always one determined to face in an opposite direction from the way the arranger desires.

MARCELENE COX

• • • • •

You don't really understand human nature unless you know why a child on a merry-go-round will wave at his parents every time around— and why his parents will always wave back.

WILLIAM D. TAMMEUS

Parents can only give good advice or put them
on the right paths, but the final forming of a
person's character lies in their own hands.

ANNE FRANK

● ● ● ● ●

No man on his deathbed ever looked up into
the eyes of his family and friends and said,
"I wish I'd spent more time at the office."

UNKNOWN

We never know the love of our parents
for us till we have become parents.
HENRY WARD BEECHER

• • • • •

As the mother grows, and the father grows,
the children grow, and the society grows,
because we're all one piece.
ANGELA BARRON MCBRIDE

• • • • •

The wildest colts can make the best horses.
PLUTARCH

Letting go means giving up basing our own
self-worth on our children's behavior.
MELISSA GAYLE WEST

• • • • •

The most effective kind of education is that
children play among lovely things.
PLATO

• • • • •

If you want to see what children will do,
you must stop giving them things.
NORMAN DOUGLAS

To see what you have made coming forth from within you, and that moment of first version, to love it totally and for always. . . Can anyone who has not given birth, in fact or in imagination, understand what it means for God to have created us?

MARGARET HEBBLETHWAITE

There never was a child so lovely but
his mother was glad to get him asleep.
RALPH WALDO EMERSON

• • • • •

It is. . .a lifelong process of discovery, a cycle
that will be repeated, in various degrees of
intensity and increasing depth, whenever our
children enter a new developmental phase.
MELISSA GAYLE WEST

Every [parent] knows reverence at the creation
of her newborn baby, who is so obviously
a person from the first moment she sees him.
More reverence still would a [parent] feel if she
could already see with the eyes of God all that
her child would grow to—the talent and beauty
and strength and love that are already
written into his makeup.

MARGARET HEBBLETHWAITE

Parents often talk about the younger generation as if they didn't have anything to do with it.
HAIM GINOTT

The trouble with learning to parent on
the job is that your child is the teacher.
ROBERT BRAULT

• • • • •

If you have never been hated by your child,
you have never been a parent.
BETTE DAVIS

If you want children to keep their feet
on the ground, put some responsibility
on their shoulders.
ABIGAIL VAN BUREN

• • • • •

The quickest way for a parent to get a child's
attention is to sit down and look comfortable.
LANE OLINGHOUSE

It kills you to see them grow up. But I guess
it would kill you quicker if they didn't.
BARBARA KINGSOLVER

• • • • •

Children are a great comfort in your old age—
and they help you reach it faster, too.
LIONEL KAUFFMAN

• • • • •

Most of us become parents long before
we have stopped being children.
MIGNON MCLAUGHLIN

If there is anything that we wish to change in the child, we should first examine it and see whether it is not something that could better be changed in ourselves.

C. G. Jung

• • • • •

Simply having children does not make mothers.

John A. Shedd

Although there are many trial marriages. . .
there is no such thing as a trial child.
GAIL SHEEHY

• • • • •

Your children tell you casually years later
what it would have killed you with
worry to know at the time.
MIGNON MCLAUGHLIN

The beauty of "spacing" children many years apart lies in the fact that parents have time to learn the mistakes that were made with the older ones—which permits them to make exactly the opposite mistakes with the younger ones.

S<small>YDNEY</small> J. H<small>ARRIS</small>

My mom used to say it doesn't matter how many kids you have . . .because one kid'll take up 100 percent of your time, so more kids can't possibly take up more than 100 percent of your time.

KAREN BROWN

What a child doesn't receive
he can seldom later give.
P. D. JAMES

• • • • •

If your children spend most of their time in
other people's houses, you're lucky; if they all
congregate at your house, you're blessed.
MIGNON MCLAUGHLIN

• • • • •

Now the thing about having a baby—
and I can't be the first person to have
noticed this—is that thereafter you have it.
JEAN KERR

How pleasant it is for a father to sit at his child's board. It is like an aged man reclining under the shadow of an oak which he has planted.

WALTER SCOTT

• • • • •

You will always be your child's favorite toy.

VICKI LANSKY

Give me the life of the boy whose mother is nurse, seamstress, washerwoman, cook, teacher, angel, and saint, all in one, and whose father is guide, exemplar, and friend. No servants to come between. These are the boys who are born to the best fortune.

ANDREW CARNEGIE

• • • • •

Never raise your hand to your kids.
It leaves you unprotected.

RED BUTTONS

Kids spell love T-I-M-E.
JOHN CRUDELE

• • • • •

There may be some doubt as to who are the best
people to have charge of children, but there can
be no doubt that parents are the worst.
GEORGE BERNARD SHAW

• • • • •

A parent who has never apologized to his
children is a monster. If he's always
apologizing, his children are monsters.
MIGNON MCLAUGHLIN

The guys who fear becoming fathers don't understand that fathering is not something perfect men do, but something that perfects the man. The end product of child raising is not the child but the parent.

FRANK PITTMAN

• • • • •

If nature had arranged that husbands and wives should have children alternatively, there would never be more than three in a family.

LAWRENCE HOUSMAN

As parents, we guide by our unspoken
example. It is only when we're talking
to them that our kids aren't listening.

ROBERT BRAULT

• • • • •

Mother Nature is wonderful. Children get too
old for piggy-back rides just about the same
time they get too heavy for them.

UNKNOWN

I don't believe professional athletes should be role models. I believe parents should be role models. . . . It's not like it was when I was growing up. My mom and my grandmother told me how it was going to be. If I didn't like it, they said, "Don't let the door hit you on the way out." Parents have to take better control.

CHARLES BARKLEY

• • • • •

The child supplies the power; but the parents have to do the steering.

BENJAMIN SPOCK